ARTIST FOCUS #04

甫木元空

窓外 1991-2021

Sora Hokimoto

inter face 1991-2021

2023年12月16日—2024年2月18日

December 16, 2023 - February 18, 2024

ごあいさつ

このたび高知県立美術館では、ジャンルや年齢を問わず、学芸員が推薦した高知ゆかりの作家を紹介する展覧会シリーズ「ARTIST FOCUS」の第4回として、映画作家・甫木元空（1992〜）の個展を開催いたします。

自らの両親の死を契機に、甫木元はドキュメンタリーとフィクションを掛け合わせる手法で、「身近な人の不在／喪失」や「不在への向き合い方」といった普遍的なテーマを扱ってきました。このテーマを引き継ぐ本展は、展示という枠組みを用いて、映画作家が私的な「記憶」と外的な「記録」の関係性を問い直す試みです。

2017年に甫木元は関東を離れ、祖父と母が住む高知県四万十町へと移住しました。その後病身の母を看取った21年までの約4年間、まるで日記をつけるかのように家族との日常をスマートフォンやフィルムカメラで記録します。そうして撮影したある種の家族写真と、生前の父と母が甫木元の誕生以前の91年から撮りはじめたホームビデオが、本展の出品作品を構成する主な素材です。
少しずつ病み衰えていく母の姿と、健やかに成長していく子どもの姿。死と生に向かうそれぞれの旅路が収められた記録は、編集を通じてドキュメンタリーからフィクションへと変化します。本来の文脈から引き離して再構成された記録は、あたかも作家自身の記憶を繋ぎ合わせたロードムービーのように、新たな意味をもって私たちの前に現れるのです。

展覧会名の「窓外」における「窓」という言葉に、甫木元はこちらとあちら、ひいてはこの世とあの世を隔てる境界のイメージを重ねています。「窓の外」に旅立った故人の面影を編み直し、新たな表現の回路を拓こうとする作家の試みを、この機会にぜひご体感ください。

最後になりましたが、本展の開催にあたり、さまざまな形でご助力を賜りました各団体・各社の皆様に、この場を借りて心より感謝申し上げます。

高知県立美術館

窓外 1991-2021

甫木元空

2017年に祖父が暮らす高知に移住し、余命宣告された母の残された時間を記録に残せないかと、2017年から2021年にかけて撮りためた母の写真。父が残した自分が生まれる数ヶ月前から始まる、1991年から1992年の母の映像。

人が生まれ死んでいく、始まりと終わりの物語を映像と写真、一筆書きで物語る事はできないのかと思い、構想したのが今回の展示の始まりです。

記憶、記録、家族。気づけば共に生活していく中で、それまで母に一度もカメラを向けた事がありませんでした。

誰しもが死を迎える瞬間もう少しだけ生きてくれたらと願う夢を、「はだかのゆめ」と名づけて、記憶ではなく確かな足跡を残すため母の気配と当時残していたメモを元に映画、音楽、小説と作品を作りました。そこにいたはずの気配と当時残していたメモを元に記憶を再構築していく作業。

自然の中の死は平然といつでも横たわっているもので、母の死後、風景

はいつも通り、何事もなかったかの様に変わらずそこにただあり続け、
季節はいつも通りすぎさっていきます。
普通に歩いていた母が、ある時から杖を突き始め、髪が抜けていき、帽
子を被るようになっても、ウド、タケノコ、イチゴ、きし豆茶、餅……例
年通り季節と共に作物は実り枯れていきました。

どんなに大事な人であっても月日が経つうちに忘れていくし、波のよう
に唐突に思い出される事もあれば、はなからいなかったかの様な感覚に
さえなる時があります。風景、季節に母が溶けていくまでの月日。

順路をたどりながら自分のリズムで編集して繋ぎ止めながら見る写真の
イメージ。それぞれが覗き込んだ窓外の風景が、父が撮影したホームビ
デオの映像から聞こえてくる亡き王女のためのパヴァーヌと重なる時、
次の季節へと繋がる軌跡となって見えてくれたら嬉しいです。

目次 | Contents

窓外

Sceneries Outside the Window

11

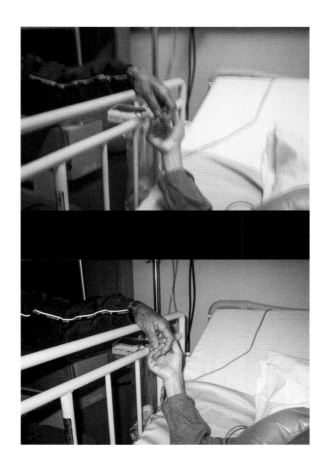

1

2

3

4

5

6

7

8

9

10

11

12

13

14

15

16

17

18

19

20

21

22

23

24

1991

1992 3 2

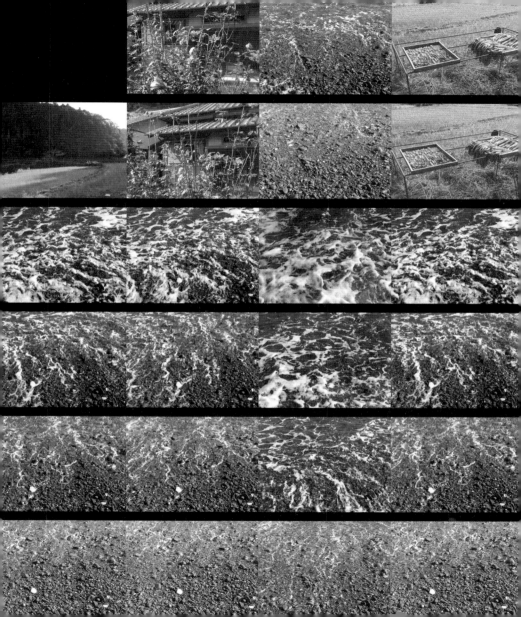

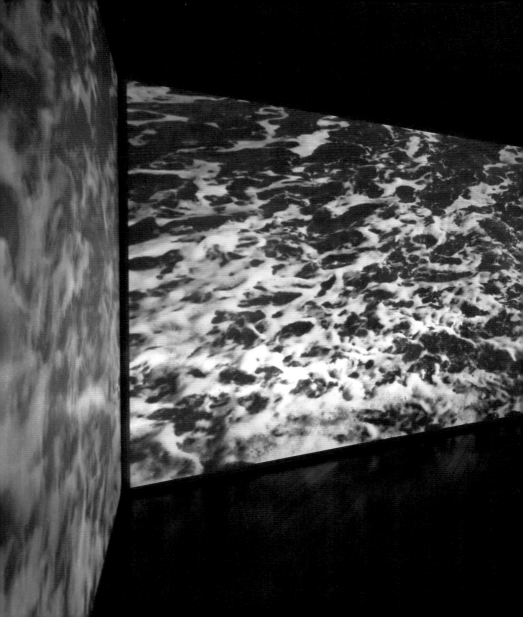

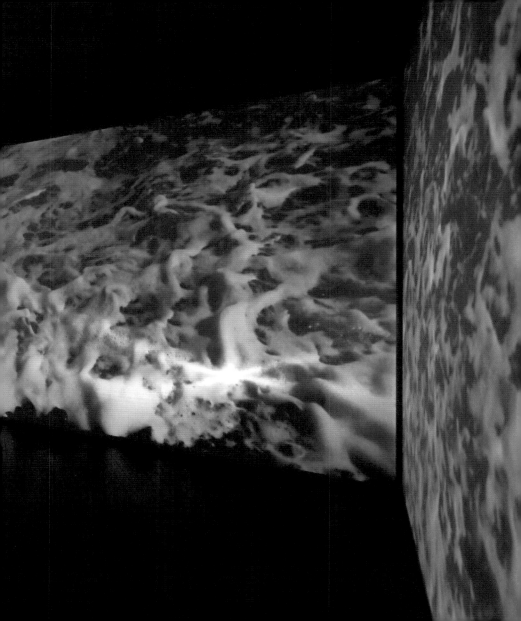

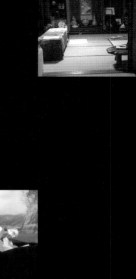

銀河
Galaxy

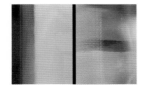

窓外 inter face 1991-2021

甫木元空 Sora Hokimoto

窓の外へ──甫木元空論

塚本麻莉（高知県立美術館主任学芸員）

　蝉の抜け殻、洗濯物の揺れ、いつまでも帰らないカエル、土と喧嘩する様に
耕す祖父、容赦無く打ちつける荒波、ただただ風に身を任せ揺れるネムノキ、
抵抗せず沈む事を前提に作られた沈下橋、全てを洗濯するような雨。物語よ
り饒舌なこの風景を記録し、残したい。

甫木元空『はだかのゆめ』あとがきより

　映画、音楽、小説。多岐にわたる媒体を介して、甫木元空は繰り返し肉親
の死に向き合ってきた。たとえば甫木元の監督映画である『終わりのな
い歌』と『はるねこ』は父の、『はだかのゆめ』は母の死を契機に手掛けた
「弔い映画」であった[1]。本展「窓外 1991-2021」は、母の死を主題に据え
た点でこれらと同様の系譜に連なるものだ。

経歴

はじめに、甫木元の生い立ちとこれまでの主な活動を時系列に沿って確
認しておこう。
　1992年、音楽講師の母と市民ミュージカル演出家の父との間に生まれた
甫木元は、二人兄弟の長男として埼玉県入間郡越生町で育った。劇団に
所属する傍ら作曲も行っていた母と、演劇の世界で活動し、埼玉を拠点

に戦争や政治・社会問題を題材とする劇作を手掛けた父の生き方は、今なお作家の表現の根底を支えている。

2010年、甫木元は多摩美術大学映像演劇学科に進学し、12年に教授として赴任した教授・映画監督の青山真治と出会って転機を迎えた。父の死をきっかけに取り組んだ卒業制作の監督映画『終わりのない歌』は青山から高く評価され、卒業後はそのプロデュースのもと、初の長編監督作『はるねこ』を制作する。脚本と音楽も担当し、16年に公開した『はるねこ』は国内外で上映される機会を得た。一方の私生活では、母が癌で余命宣告を受けたことをきっかけに、17年に母と祖父が暮らす四万十町へと移住する。

移住後は、「ビキニ事件²」を取り上げた劇を構想していた父の遺志を引き継ぐように高知県在住の事件関係者への取材をはじめ、ドキュメンタリー映画の制作や個展を行っている。また、19年に結成したバンドBialystocksは22年にメジャーデビューを果たし、以降は音楽活動も本格化させた。21年の母の死を受けて制作した監督映画『はだかのゆめ』は翌年に公開となったほか、同名の小説も刊行している。

ふたつの映画と「距離」

映画作家、ミュージシャン、小説家。複数の肩書きをもつ甫木元だが、表現の主軸となるのは映画である。したがって、「窓外 1991-2021」展は映画作家が展覧会というメディアを通じて挑んだ、映画表現の変奏だと捉えることができる。そこで、まずは甫木元による過去の監督作『終わりのない歌』(2014)と『はだかのゆめ』(2022)の概要を振り返っておく。家族の喪失を扱う両作には、主題やモティーフにおいて本展との共通点が

見られるからだ。

『終わりのない歌』は、2013年に逝去した父が残したホームビデオのフッテージを用いたセミドキュメンタリーである。この映画では、父が撮影した幼少期の甫木元兄弟の日常を捉えたビデオパートと、成長した兄弟の生活を役者が再現した劇中劇のフィクションパートとが交互に繋がれ、父と息子、それぞれの視線が交錯する造りとなっている。

他方、祖父や逝去した母の言葉を脚本執筆の手がかりにしたという『はだかのゆめ』では、甫木元の実際の家族構成を反映した祖父、母、息子からなる一家の人々が登場する。母と息子は役者が演じたが、祖父役には甫木元の実の祖父が当てられ、主な撮影地も四万十町の実家やその周辺であった。しかし物語自体は、母と過ごした日々の記憶を、映画的想像力に根ざしたフィクションへと昇華したものだ。具体的にいうと、劇中では母と息子の状態が現実とは逆転している。すなわち母は病を抱えつつ「この世」を生き、息子は「あの世」に属しながらも「この世」をさまよう。本作では生者としての母と死者としての息子との間に横たわる物理的、状況的、心情的な「距離」が、火振り漁や沈下橋、四国カルストといった高知の風物を背景に描かれている。

人間は他者との距離を測りながら関係性を築く。そうした人対人の関係性を一方的に断ち切るのが死だ。これらの映画に共通するのは、ホームビデオといった記録や実在の場所・人物といった「本当（現実）のこと」に創作要素を掛け合わせる演出手法だけではない。現実の親との関係を死によって絶たれた作家が、創作を通して故人と自らとの間の距離を測り直し、両者の関係の再構築を試みた点もまた、共通する特徴のひとつに挙げられるだろう。

「窓外 1991-2021」展

ふたつの映画では、故人と自らを隔てる「距離」の描写が重要な位置を占めていた。それはこの展覧会においても例外ではない。「距離を描きたい」——本展準備のために行った打ち合わせで、幾度となく甫木元が話した言葉を筆者は覚えている。

『はだかのゆめ』と同様、展示で「母の死」を取り上げることは早い段階で決定した。ただし展覧会は映画とは異なり、物理的な場所と空間を伴うメディアだ。甫木元はこうした展覧会の特性を活かして、自らの手元に残された「記録」だけを用いて作品を展開させるプランを最終的に提案した。

高知に移住してからの甫木元は、余命宣告を受けた母の姿を残すため、家族とのささやかな日常を映像や写真で日記のように撮り溜めていたという。そのように蓄積した記録を自らの個人的な「記憶」を描く媒体にして、展覧会場を他者と記憶を共有する場とすること。それが本展のコンセプトとなった。

さらに、甫木元が選んだ距離を象徴するモティーフが「窓」である。記号的な意味での窓は、場所や空間、時間を分かつ境界として機能する。したがって、本展と作品の名称に採用された言葉「窓外」は、文字通りの意味に加えて「あの世」の比喩とも理解されうる[3]。

以降は本展の作品について具体的に見ていこう。「窓外 1991-2021」展は〈窓外〉、〈1991〉、〈銀河〉の3作品から構成されている。

窓外

〈窓外〉は、甫木元の母が亡くなる前後までの日々を、高知の風景とともに描いた写真連作だ。登場するのは母のほか同居する祖父、時折訪ねてくる弟、弟夫婦の間に誕生した姪である。特に中盤から登場する幼い姪は、闘病で弱っていく母と対比をなす存在として、世代の交代、さらには生と死が地続きの事象であることを鑑賞者に意識させる。また、実家近くの畦道で枝を伸ばすネムノキや軒先の物干し竿、飛沫を上げる海といったイメージは、繰り返し現れて季節の移り変わりを示すとともに、物語に詩的な余韻を与えている。

なお、本作の素材となったのは、先述のとおり甫木元が移住した2017年から母が逝去した21年初頭までに撮り溜めたスナップ写真である。プリント1枚につき2つのイメージが含まれているのは、撮影にハーフサイズカメラを用いたことに由来する[4]。

この作品を読み解く手がかりとなるのが、「モンタージュ（編集）」と呼ばれる映画技法だ。これは映画や映像編集で、異なるショットやシーンを組み合わせて特定の感情や意味を創造する技法である。本作では額装された72枚のプリントが配置されているため、シリーズ全体では144のイメージが並ぶ計算になる。だから次のように考えるとわかりやすい。甫木元は自らが撮影したスナップ写真から144のイメージを選び、それらを対にして72組にしたうえで、映像編集と同様の感覚で壁面にモンタージュしたのだ、と。

こうしたプロセスは、イメージがもつ記録性よりも新たな文脈や視覚上のリズムをつくるための編集が優先されたことを意味する。よって必然的に、〈窓外〉におけるイメージの並びは厳密な時系列には沿っていない。

甫木元は在りし日の母の気配を効果的に浮かび上がらせるためにイメージの操作を行っている。一方でその実態については明言を避け、見る者の解釈に任せる姿勢をとる。たとえば母の葬式の後に続くイメージ（69、p.39）で、すでに亡くなったはずの母のひそやかな登場——すなわち生前に撮ったイメージが用いられている——をどう受け止めるかは、あくまで鑑賞者に委ねられている。

また、甫木元は本作のプリントを、あえて額装して提示することを選んだ。鑑賞者は整然と並んだフレームのアクリルカバー越しにイメージ群と対峙することになるが、このような額装は〈窓外〉というタイトルをメタ的に体現している。つまり鑑賞者は物理的な意味でも「窓の外」を覗き込むように、ある家族が送った日々を眺めるのだ。

1991

両親と自らが残した記録を再編して、「家族の始まりと終わり」を描いた4チャンネルのビデオ・インスタレーションが〈1991〉である。鑑賞者はスクリーンで囲まれた菱形の空間に入り、四方に投射された映像を観る。各スクリーンのサイズの大きさも相まって一度に触れる情報量は多いが、それゆえ甫木元家の記憶の中を歩くかのような没入的な体験が可能だ。本作で流れる映像は、便宜的に前半と後半に分けて考えられる。前半は2017年から21年までに甫木元がスマートフォンで撮った動画で構成され、母が病没するまでの日常を捉えた〈窓外〉のイメージと共通するシーンが多数含まれている。これに続く後半は、1991年12月から92年3月までに撮影された、甫木元の誕生前後の様子を収めたホームビデオのフッテージを編集したものだ[5]。後半は両親の撮影だそうだが、映像では母の

姿が多くを占めており、結果的に父の視線が強調される。加えて、無音の前半に対して後半からは音声が入るため、視点の切り替わりが聴覚的にも理解しやすい。特に前半の最終部は、母の死後、火葬場へと向かう霊柩車の内部を映した沈痛なシーンだ。そこにおよそ30年前、若き日の表情豊かな母の姿が抒情的な音楽の調べとともに表れると、景色は唐突に生彩を帯びる。ここでの音楽は、父が好んだモーリス・ラヴェルの「亡き王女のためのパヴァーヌ」の旋律が主体で、やはり父が撮影したビデオから甫木元が別途抽出している。

カメラワークの点でも、前半と後半では母という被写体との向き合い方に明らかな相違がある。前半では母の後ろ姿を距離を取って捉えた窃視的なショットが多かったのに対して、後半のカメラは正面から堂々と母に向けられている。母もカメラに向けてポーズを取るなど、撮影時に被写体と撮影者との間で交わされた親密なコミュニケーションが垣間見える。このような視点の差異は、死期が迫る母の姿を記録しようとする、ある種残酷にも受け取れる行為に後ろめたさを覚える息子と、出産直前の妻と誕生する子どもの姿を余さず記録しようとする父との立場の違いそのものといえる。「残したい」という同じ目的をもって同じ被写体を撮っているからこそ、両者の視点や関係、状況の違いがいっそう際立つのだ。

子と親の立場からそれぞれの死と生を描いた本作のもうひとつの特徴は、ループ再生することだ。たとえば暗いトンネルを抜けるシーンから始まる冒頭は、映像が終点から始点へとループする時に見ると、この世に誕生する胎児が通る産道にも思える。死から生へ、あるいは生から死へ。家族の記録から立ち上げた本作には、連綿と続く平凡な、それでいて普遍的な生の営みが映し出されている。

銀河

本展の締めくくりに位置する〈銀河〉は、〈窓外〉の続編にあたる写真連作だ。前提として、写真は刹那の光を介して過去の像をこの世に留める技術である。甫木元はそのことを踏まえ、「さまざまな事象が複雑に絡み合って成立するこの世の風景」の比喩として本作を提示している。また、このタイトルは四万十町の廃棄物処理施設「クリーンセンター銀河」からの引用らしい。

〈窓外〉の続編といっても、本作に用いられたイメージはそれと同じ2017年から21年にかけて撮影されており、ネムノキを除いてプリントのイメージは対になっている。姪の顔のアップ、フィルムの感光による具象的なモティーフが見出せない色彩のグラデーション、そして、これまで何度も登場してきたネムノキ。しかしこれらの散文的なイメージは〈窓外〉とは異なり、ストーリー性や意味的な繋がりが一見判然としない。

実のところ〈銀河〉におけるイメージは、ノーファインダー撮影（カメラのファインダーやディスプレイを覗かずに撮影する手法）によって得たものだ。つまり本作は、撮影者すら何が写っているかが予想できないままに撮った、従来の目的である「記録」からも外れたイメージで構成されている。

出品作の中でもっとも客観的な解釈の手がかりが少ない〈銀河〉を読み解くヒントは、このタイトルに掛けられた多義的な意味——美しい光を放つ天体とモノが行きつく最終地点であるゴミ処理場——と、本作が、母が亡くなるまでの日々を辿った〈窓外〉の続編であることに尽きるだろう。母の死の次にくる風景。それはすなわち、「母という、残したい対象が不在の風景」だと考えられる。記録対象の母はもういない。だからこそ、甫木元は予期せず手に入れた偶発的なイメージの断片を繋ぎ合わせて、母

のいない風景に生きる実感を描いた。その意味において、本作が次の世代を生きていく姪のイメージに始まり、展覧会の冒頭、〈窓外〉の1枚目と同じネムノキで終わるのは象徴的だ。しかも〈銀河〉のネムノキは冒頭での落葉した姿とは打って変わって葉が茂り花も咲いており、ここに来るまでに流れた年月をも感じさせる。

だが、よくよく考えるとネムノキが開花するのは初夏であり、母が逝去したのは冬である。〈銀河〉は〈窓外〉と同時期に撮影したものだから、展覧会の末尾に配されて、あたかも母の死後の風景のように振る舞うこのイメージは、実際には母の存命時に撮られている。ゆえに最後のネムノキには、過去と未来が二重写しにされていると考えることもできるのだ。

距離

これまでの3作品の読み解きを通じて、それらの内容が有機的に連動していることが改めて明らかとなった。俯瞰して見ると、ある家族の中で起こった死と生、そしてめぐりゆく季節が作品単位で「モンタージュ」されたこの展覧会自体を、「窓外 1991-2021」というひとつの作品とみなせるだろう。ここに来てようやく、甫木元が描こうとした「距離」が作品において具体的にどのように反映されていたのかを考える素地が整った。

甫木元の制作における距離とは、死者と生者との間に横たわる隔たりのことだと筆者はすでに述べた。これを本展の作品に照らして考えると、その描写は主に「記録対象の可視化／不可視化」の調整によって行われてきたことが浮かび上がる。甫木元の作品に用いられたイメージやフッテージの多くは、家族と過ごした日常のワンシーンを捉えた何気ないものだ。一方で、一般的な家族写真やホームビデオでは撮らないはずのお

びただしい量の風景のほか、病院や霊柩車の内部にまでカメラを向けている点は特異だといえる。しかし、作品上での「母の見せ方」だけは一貫していた。たとえば〈窓外〉では、母の表情を捉えたイメージは50 (p.29)を最後に姿を消し、その死は葬儀の風景 (62、p.35) によって鑑賞者に知らされた。

かつて写真家の荒木経惟が妻・陽子の死に際して棺の中にまでシャッターを切り、そのイメージを大衆に供したのとは対照的に、実際に撮影したかはさておき、甫木元は棺に安置された母の遺体は決して見せようとしなかった。死にまつわる直接的な言及を避け、葬儀の前後や母のいない屋内外の風景を通じて、母の死に伴う孤独や喪失感を間接的に描くことに留めたのだった。

「愛する者の死」という主題は、古今東西の芸術家が取り組んできた、ある種ありふれたものだ。そのような主題をもとに、新たな表現を立ち上げるのは決して容易ではない。写真家としての技量はいうまでもなく、時には社会通念や倫理的なタブーをかなぐり捨ててでも撮らざるを得なかった、「病」に蝕まれたともいえる荒木のように直接性へと振り切らないのであれば、死から距離を取って客観的な視点を担保するしかない。そのような距離は「余白」と言い換えることもできるだろう。本展の場合、挿入された数々の風景や祖父、弟、姪といった母以外の登場人物が、いや、イメージに置き換えられた母自身もが、物語を牽引しながら余白の役割をも果たしていた。

誤解を恐れずにいうと、甫木元による写真の個々のイメージは、構図やピントの合わせ方といった技術的な側面が殊更に秀でているわけではない。それでいて写真と映像、いずれの媒体においても、被写体との親密な関係性は的確に定着されている。だからこそ本展における数多のイメージは

親しみやすく、鑑賞者の感情移入を許容する余白をもつ。

巧みな配置と連続性、それとは不釣り合いなイメージの弱さ——アマチュア性が鑑賞者とイメージとの距離を架橋し、鑑賞者が物語の余白に入り込み、結果的に「自分ごと」として共感する余地を与えているという側面も指摘できるだろう。

結び

従来の「アート」の世界では、病的であったり、センセーショナルであったり、タブーすら乗り越える非常識な作家の振る舞いは決して否定されるものではなかった。そのことを考慮すると、今回の甫木元の表現は、健康的で、凡庸で、通俗的といえるかもしれない。甫木元は編集した記録を通じて直接性を回避しながら母の死を扱い、最後まで詩的な情趣を維持したまま作品を展開させた。言い換えると、際どいところで母を不躾な鑑賞者——他者の視線から遮蔽しつつ、同時に自らの記憶を他者と共有する術を探ったのであった。平凡な日々の中に潜む詩性をごく個人的な視点から見出し、抽出して構成してみせるところにこそ、この作家の面白さがある。

他方で、音楽活動を通して自らがスポットを浴びる甫木元がこうした題材を取り上げると、それ自体が感情移入の対象として消費される危うさがつきまとう。筆者はアートが消費の対象とされること自体を批判する立場ではないが、ひとつ確かなのは、優れた芸術作品の多くが永遠を志向するのとは裏腹に、属人的な共感で大衆の支持を得る作品や活動の賞味期限は短いということだ。

だが、甫木元は自らが消費の対象となり得るリスクも理解する傍らで、

肉親の死を「残したい」という欲望に忠実に振る舞い、『終わりのない歌』の時点から一貫してベタな欲望を自己参照的に処理し、自らの表現へと変換してきた。大衆性と芸術性のいずれにも振り切らないで、最後には自らの内面で生起する個人的な感覚を最優先させてしまう部分が、筆者が知る限りの甫木元の表現に通底する作家性である。

ところで、筆者は先日興味深い本を読んだ。故人が登場する夢を見た遺族の多くは、夢を「見る」のではなく、故人に「見せられている」とする受け身の立場で夢を解釈するのだそうだ[6]。これを踏まえると、窓の外を見るのは主体の意志が要求される、能動的な行為であるといえる。『はだかのゆめ』から「窓外」へと続いてきた死者——母と自らの間の距離を探る旅は、実際の記録を素材に用いた本展において頂点に達し、同時に行き場を見失ったように見える。〈銀河〉のネムノキが過去でも現在でも未来でもない場所で、何事かのはじまりか、あるいは終わりを告げるような余韻だけを残して行んでいたように。
甫木元の次なる課題は、故人の記憶と喪失の痛みを抱えたまま、それでも「窓の外」へと一歩を踏み出すことだろう。これからも続く作家の旅路の先で振り返った時、本展は新たな出発点に見えるだろうか。

---

1 甫木元空「ディレクターズ・インタビュー」『はだかのゆめ』（映画パンフレット）2022年、株式会社boid, pp.7-8

2 1954年、マーシャル諸島ビキニ環礁・エニウェトク環礁で行われた米国の水爆実験で発生した放射性降下物により、第五福竜丸をはじめとした多くの日本漁船が汚染マグロを廃棄させられた事件。

3 展覧会名としての「窓外」の訳語は、翻訳家のアンドレアス・シュトゥールマンの提案を受けて「inter face」の表記とした。接頭辞「inter」(間／相互に)と「face」(面／向き合う)を意図的に分けることで、「異なる面が相互に向き合う」という感覚を強調し、物理的な隔たりを視覚的に表している。

4 甫木元が撮影に使用したのは、「オリンパスペンS」である。ただし、甫木元は撮影したフィルムをデジタル化し、PC上でイメージの順番を並べ替えた後、最終的にプリントとして出力している。

5 〈1991〉には、1992年に原爆の図 丸木美術館で撮影された、丸木位里・丸木俊による〈原爆の図〉の画像が含まれる (p.58の上から3段目の右端と右から3つ目、上から4段目の右から3つ目の画像)。

6 金菱清「孤立 "夢" 援——なぜ震災後、亡き人と夢で邂逅するのか」『私の夢まで、会いに来てくれた 3・11 亡き人とのそれから』2021年、朝日新聞出版、pp.222-242

参考文献・ウェブサイト一覧

荒木経惟 (著・写真)、東京都写真美術館 (監修)『荒木経惟 センチメンタルな旅 1971-2017-』2017年、HeHe

甫木元空『その次の季節 高知県被曝者の肖像』2021年、this and that

東北学院大学 震災の記録プロジェクト 金菱清 (ゼミナール)『私の夢まで、会いに来てくれた 3・11 亡き人とのそれから』2021年、朝日新聞出版

『はだかのゆめ』(映画パンフレット) 2022年、株式会社boid

甫木元空『はだかのゆめ』2023年、新潮社

「若手監督インタビュー『終わりのない歌』甫木元空監督 (文・深田隆之)」
https://umi-theater.jimdofree.com/interview-owari/ (2024年2月6日閲覧)

「甫木元空に聞く、『窓外 1991-2021』の狙い。記録写真を「動く映画」にするまで。(文・金原由佳)」https://madamefigaro.jp/culture/231229-artistfocus04.html (2024年2月6日閲覧)

映画

『終わりのない歌』監督・脚本：甫木元空、2014年、68分

『はだかのゆめ』監督・脚本・編集：甫木元空、2022年、59分

略歴
Biography

甫木元空（ほきもと・そら）
1992年、埼玉県生まれ。2014年、多摩美術大学映像演劇学科卒業。在学中に教授の映画監督・青山真治を通して映画に触れる。主な監督映画に『はるねこ』、『はだかのゆめ』などがある。音楽活動やMV制作も行い、19年にバンドBialystocksを結成、ボーカルおよび作詞作曲を担当する。20年には須崎市のアート事業「現代地方譚」の総合ディレクターを務めた。映画をベースに音楽制作などジャンルにとらわれない活動を続ける。

主な映画
2016年『はるねこ』＊第46回ロッテルダム国際映画祭コンペティション部門出品
2022年『はだかのゆめ』＊第35回東京国際映画祭 Nippon Cinema Now部門正式招待

書籍
『その次の季節 高知県被曝者の肖像』2021年、this and that
『はだかのゆめ』2023年、新潮社

個展
2021年
「その次の季節」（すさきまちかどギャラリー/旧三浦邸、高知）
2023年
「ARTIST FOCUS #04 甫木元空 窓外 1991-2021」（高知県立美術館、高知）

Hokimoto Sora
Born 1992 in Saitama. Graduated from Tama Art University, Department of Moving Images and Performing Arts in 2014. During his studies, he was introduced to filmmaking through his professor, the film director Shinji Aoyama. Film works include "Haruneko" and "Visit Me in My Dreams." Also makes music and produces music videos, among others as a singer/songwriter for the band "Bialystocks" that he formed in 2019. In 2020, he was the general director for "Contemporary tales from the province 8," a local art program in Susaki City. Based on expression through film, he continues to engage in cross-genre activities such as music production.

Selected Filmography
2016 Haruneko *Selected for the Competition at the 46th International Film Festival Rotterdam
2022 Visit Me in My Dreams *Officially invited film to the 35th Tokyo International Film Festival's "Nippon Cinema Now" section

Books
The Next Chapter – Portraits of Hibakusha in Kochi (2021, this and that)
Hadaka no yume (2023, Shinchosha Publishing Co., Ltd.)

Solo Exhibition
2021
The Next Chapter (Susaki Machikado Gallery / Former Miura House, Kochi)
2023
ARTIST FOCUS #04 Sora Hokimoto inter face 1991-2021 (The Museum of Art, Kochi, Kochi)

作品リスト
List of Works

窓外
全72点
2023年、インクジェットプリント
各35.6×27.0 cm
作家蔵

1991
2023年、ビデオ・インスタレーション（4面/カラー）
6分43秒（ループ再生）
作家蔵

銀河
全6点
2023年、インクジェットプリント
各35.6×27.0 cm
作家蔵

Sceneries Outside the Window
Total of 72 works
2023, inkjet print
35.6×27.0 cm each
Collection of the artist

1991
2023, video installation (4 channels/color)
6 min 43 sec (loop)
Collection of the artist

Galaxy
Total of 6 works
2023, inkjet print
35.6×27.0 cm each
Collection of the artist

pp. 80-81　〈銀河〉より　From the series *Galaxy*

Introduction

The Museum of Art, Kochi announces volume 4 in the "ARTIST FOCUS" series of exhibitions introducing selected artists of all ages and genres, that are associated with Kochi in one way or another. The exhibition this time focuses on the work of filmmaker Sora Hokimoto (born 1992).

The passing of his parents inspired Hokimoto to adopt such universal themes as "the absence/loss of someone close" and "how to deal with absence," to the works he creates by combining elements of documentary and fiction. These are also the general themes at this exhibition, the idea behind which was to have the filmmaker utilize the format of exhibits to explore the relationships between personal "memories" and public "records."

In 2017, Hokimoto left the Kanto region, and relocated to Shimanto in Kochi, where his grandfather and his mother lived. For the next four years, until 2021, he used his smartphone and film camera to record in a diary style his daily family life while nursing his sickly mother. The resulting "family album," along with home videos that his parents had started shooting in 1991, before Hokimoto's birth, are the centerpieces that this exhibition was conceived around. On the one side, there is his mother and her gradually declining physical condition, and on the other, children growing up healthy. These two journeys, heading toward death and life respectively, are captured in a work that is edited to transform from a documentary into a fictional style. Isolated from their original contexts and recombined, the images present themselves with entirely new meanings, almost like a road movie that tells a story based on its creator's memory.

The exhibition's title "inter face" reflects the image of a window (as in the Japanese title) which Hokimoto interprets as a "double-faced" divider between two realms – in this case also meaning this life and the afterlife. The exhibition will be an opportunity to witness the artist explore a new avenue for his creative work, as he reimagines a deceased person and her journey "on this and the other side of the window."

Finally, we would like to express our heartfelt thanks to all individuals, organizations and corporations involved, for their various support in the realization of this exhibition.

The Museum of Art, Kochi

inter face 1991-2021

Sora Hokimoto

In 2017, I moved to Kochi where my grandfather was living, driven by the desire to somehow capture the remaining time that my mother had been given to live by her doctor. This resulted in a series of photographs of my mother, taken between 2017 and 2021. Then there are videos of her that my father had made in 1991-92, starting a few months prior to my own birth.

My idea was to work out a way of creating some sort of narrative from photographs and videos, that illustrates how people are born and die, and how everything has a beginning and an end. This is the basic concept from which the plan for this exhibition developed.

When reflecting on memories, records, and my family, it occurred to me that I had never pointed my camera at my mother during the time we lived together.

Whenever someone dies, we always wish he or she would be around for just a little bit longer. That wish, or dream, I called "Hadaka no yume" (literally "naked dream")*, and in order to produce not only memories but something tangible that remains, I began to make a movie, music, and a novel, based on the lingering sensation of my mother's presence, and notes that I had taken during her lifetime. So it was an operation of reconstructing memories based on notes and the sensation of someone who was supposed to be there.

Death, in nature, is something that is always lying around silently, and after my mother's death, the scenery looked just like it always did. It remained exactly the same, as if nothing at all had happened, and the months kept coming and going as usual.

At some point, my mother had begun to use a walking cane, and wear a hat because her hair had started falling out. But even then, crops continued to grow and die with each season, just like in any other year. Udo, bamboo shoots, strawberries, Kishimame tea, rice cakes...

Even the most beloved person, we gradually forget as time passes. There are moments when our memory of them suddenly revisits us like a massive wave, and others when it almost seems as if they had never existed. The days went by as my mother slowly dissolved into the surrounding sceneries and seasons, and while looking at her photographs that were left behind, I patched together the path of her life, in my own rhythm.

Whenever the "Sceneries outside the window" that each of these works present, overlap with the "Pavane pour une infante défunte" that plays in my father's home video, I hope they will make visible a new path that leads into a new chapter.

*The movie's English title is "Visit Me in My Dreams" https://hadakanoyume.com/#modal

Out of the Window – Sora Hokimoto

Mari Tsukamoto (Curator, The Museum of Art, Kochi)

> Cicada shells, laundry hung out to dry, a frog that would sit there forever, grandfather plowing the earth as if fighting with it, mercilessly beating waves, a silk tree swaying in the wind, a bridge that is flooded without resisting, and rain that seems to wash everything clean. These sceneries speak more than words. That is why I captured them in my work.
>
> Translated from Sora Hokimoto, *Hadaka no yume* (postscript)

Sora Hokimoto has been processing the death of his parents through artworks in various formats and media, including movies, music, novels, and others. He made *A Song That Never Ends* and *Haruneko* as "mourning movies" when his father passed away, and *Hadaka no yume (Visit Me in My Dreams)* after the death of his mother.[1] The exhibition "inter face 1991-2021" marks a continuation of that theme, as it revolves all around the passing of the artist's mother.

Career

Let me begin by outlining Hokimoto's personal history and artistic activities to date in chronological order.

Sora Hokimoto was born in 1992 as the first of two sons to a community theater director and his wife, a music teacher. He grew up in Ogose-machi, Iruma-gun, Saitama. The lifestyle of his parents – his mother composing music while also being a member of a theater troupe, and his father working as a Saitama-based creator of theater pieces dealing with themes of war, politics and society – is what has inspired and defined his own creative work up to this day.

In 2010, Hokimoto entered the Department of Moving Images and Performing Arts at Tama Art University, where he met the filmmaker Shinji Aoyama, who assumed a post as a professor at the university in 2012. This encounter marked a turning point in Hokimoto's career. *A Song That Never Ends*, a movie that he directed as his graduation work shortly after his father's death, was rated highly by Aoyama, who went on to produce Hokimoto's first feature-length film *Haruneko* after his graduation. The movie, for which Hokimoto wrote the script and music, was first unveiled in 2016, after which it was shown at several occasions in Japan and abroad. In private life, after the doctors had diagnosed cancer and calculated his mother's life expectancy, in 2017 Hokimoto decided to move to Shimanto-cho, where his mother and grandfather were living.

After his relocation, in honor of his father's plans to stage a theater play on the theme of the "Bikini Incident,"[2] Hokimoto conducted interviews with Kochi residents who were involved in the incident, which he eventually made into a documentary movie and a solo exhibition. When Bialystocks, the band that he had started in 2019, signed to a major label in 2022, Hokimoto began to focus more on his musical activities. The movie *Hadaka no yume* that he made after his mother's death in '21, as well as a novel with the same title, were unveiled in the following year.

Two movies and the aspect of "distance"

Although Sora Hokimoto is active as a movie director, musician and novelist, filmmaking remains the centerpiece of his creative work. Therefore, "inter face 1991-2021" can be understood as a filmmaker's attempt at a variation on the movie format in the setting of an exhibition. Let me first revisit Hokimoto's previous movies, *A Song That Never Ends* (2014) and *Hadaka no yume* (2022), as both of them deal with the loss of family members, and thus share subjects and motifs with this exhibition.

A Song That Never Ends is a semidocumentary that contains footage from home videos that his father had made up to his passing in 2013. Structured so that the perspectives of father and son intersect, this movie is composed of video parts showing the young Hokimoto and his brother in private life scenes captured by his father, alternating with fictional parts that, as a play within a play of sorts, recreate with the help of actors the grown-up brothers' daily life.

Hadaka no yume, the script for which was reportedly inspired by the words of Hokimoto's grandfather and his deceased mother, features a family of grandfather, mother and son, reflecting the artist's own family. While the mother and the son are played by actors, in the role of the grandfather is Hokimoto's real grandfather. The movie was mainly shot in the Shimanto area around the artist's family's house. His memories of the days he spent living with his mother, however, Hokimoto elaborated into a fictional story informed by cinematic imagination. Concretely speaking, in the movie, the circumstances of mother and son are reversed: the mother, although ill, still lives in "this world," while the son is visiting from his own place in the "afterworld." In the work, the physical, mental and situational "distance" between the living mother and the dead son is portrayed against the backdrops of familiar Kochi sceneries such as torch-fishing, a bridge designed to be underwater during flood, and the Shikoku Karst highlands.

People build relationships with others while assessing the distance between them. Death is the event that arbitrarily breaks such interpersonal relationships. What these movies have in common, is not only the technique that was applied in their making, namely combining "real people, places and events" captured on home videos, and creative elements. In both cases, the creative act is for the artist an act of reassessing the distance, and reestablishing the relationships between himself and his deceased parents, after their real-life relations were cut by their respective deaths.

In the two movies, the depiction of the "distance" that separates the artist from his deceased parents, plays a central role. The same applies also to this exhibition. I remember very well how Hokimoto repeatedly mentioned his desire to "depict distance" in the briefing sessions prior to the exhibition.

He had decided at an early stage to theme the exhibition on his mother's death, just like *Hadaka no yume*. However, different from a movie, an exhibition is a format that involves physical places and spaces. Hokimoto eventually proposed to create the works for display eclusively from the recordings he had collected, while utilizing the characteristics of the exhibition format.

Since his relocation to Kochi, Hokimoto had been filming and photographing scenes of daily life with his family in the style of a diary, aiming to capture his mother during the remaining time she had been given to live. The resulting footage, he used as a medium for visualizing his own personal memories, while regarding the exhibition venue as a place for sharing his memories with others. This became the underlying concept for this exhibition.

Furthermore, Hokimoto chose the "window" motif as a symbol for distance. Symbolically, a window functions as a boundary that separates places, spaces or times. In addition to the literal meaning "outside the window," the expression "窓外" in the Japanese titles of the work and the exhibition is thus also to be understood as a metaphor for the "other world (or afterworld)."[3]

Let me continue with an introduction to the three works that are featured at the "inter face 1991-2021" exhibition: *Sceneries Outside the Window*, *1991* and *Galaxy*.

Sceneries Outside the Window

Sceneries Outside the Window is a series of photographs in which Hokimoto captured the days before and after the passing of his mother, along with sceneries of Kochi. Appearing in these photographs, in addition to Hokimoto's mother, are his grandfather, who was living with them, and his brother, who occasionally came to visit along with his wife and their daughter. Especially the baby girl that appears in the latter half, as an antipode to the weakening mother, makes the viewer aware of the alternation of generations, and in addition, of the fact that life and death are two adjoining events. Repeatedly appearing images, such as the branches of a silk tree hanging over ridges between rice fields in the neighborhood, clothes poles at the eaves, and the splashing sea, reflect the turning of the seasons, while charging the story with a poetic suggestiveness.

The basic components in this series are snap photographs taken between 2017, when Hokimoto moved to Kochi, and early '21 when his mother passed away. Hokimoto shot those photos with a half-frame camera,[4] which is why there always appear two images on one print.

One clue for interpreting this work is the so-called "montage" technique that is used for editing movies and other forms of imagery, as a way of deliberately juxtaposing different shots and scenes in order to produce specific emotions or meanings. The series comprises 72 framed prints, which means that a total of 144 images are on display. In other words, Hokimoto selected 144 images from snapshots he had taken, combined them into 72 pairs, and montaged them on a wall, by an approach comparable to that of editing together a movie.

The involvement of this process means that the creation of a new context and visual rhythm at the editing stage was given priority over the images' capacity as recording media. This is why the images in *Sceneries Outside the Window* are by necessity not sequenced in a strictly chronological order. Hokimoto manipulated the images in order to effectively visualize indications of his mother when she was still alive. At the same time, however, he avoided to include statements regarding the actual situation, to let viewers interpret the work as they like. How to read the quiet appearances of the supposedly dead mother in the images that are sequenced after her funeral (69, p. 39) – using images shot during her lifetime – is all up to the viewer.

The prints in this work, Hokimoto deliberately chose to exhibit in frames. The viewer looks at the images through the acrylic covers on the methodically arranged frames, and these frames as they are embody the series' title on a meta level. In other words, as if looking at "sceneries outside the window" also in a physical sense, the viewer takes a peek into days in the life of one family.

1991

1991 is a 4-channel video installation in which Hokimoto illustrates "the beginning and the end of a family" by reorganizing material recorded by himself and his parents. Visitors enter a rhombus-shaped space surrounded by screens, where they view video footage projected in all directions. Due also to the largeness of the screens, visitors are engulfed by overwhelming amounts of information, which is exactly what makes the exhibition such an immersive experience, as if walking inside the Hokimoto family's memories.

For convenience's sake, the imagery in this work may be divided into a first and a second half. The first half consists of videos that Hokimoto shot with his smartphone between 2017 and 2021, including numerous scenes that also appear in *Sceneries Outside the Window* that captures the time between his mother's death. For the second half, Hokimoto compiled various footage from home videos filmed before and after his birth, between December 1991 and March '92.[5] The videos in the second half were filmed by his parents, but the frequent appearances of his mother suggest that the emphasis here is mainly on his father's point of view. Furthermore, different from the silent first half, the second half includes sound, which supplements the shift in perspective also acoustically. Toward the end, the first half is dominated by footage recorded after the passing of Hokimoto's mother, including pensive scenes inside the hearse on its way to the crematory. When images of his young and vibrant mother about 30 years earlier come in accompanied by lyrical music, this abruptly adds a notion of vividness. The music here, Hokimoto extracted from the home videos that his father had shot, including especially Maurice Ravel's *Pavane pour une infante défunte,* one of his father's favorite melodies. Also in terms of camera work, there are obvious differences between the first and second half, in the way the artist approaches the subject of his mother. While many scenes in the first half are shot in a somewhat voyeuristic manner from behind and from a distance, in the second half, the mother is filmed squarely from the front. She sometimes even poses for the camera, which suggests a certain level of communication between the photographer and his subject.

This difference in perspective can be regarded as reflecting the difference between the attitude of the father, who was eager to exhaustively capture his wife shortly before giving birth, and also his newborn son, and that of the son who records his mother in the face of death, not without a certain feeling of guilt for doing something that may be seen as a cruel action. It is that very motivation of both men to "capture" aspects of the same subject, that additionally highlights the differences in terms of viewpoints, relationships and situations between them.

Another unique feature of this work, in which the artist depicts life and death from the position of the parents and their child respectively, is that it is played in a loop. The film begins with a scene shot while passing through a dark tunnel, and when looped so that the playback restarts with this tunnel scene immediately after the actual end, it seems like a metaphor for the birth canal that a baby passes through when it is born. The movie proceeds from death to birth, or from birth to death. Originating from the private recordings of a family, the work reflects the endless cycle of anonymous, universal life.

Galaxy

The exhibition closes with the *Galaxy* series that was conceived as a sequel to *Sceneries Outside the Window*, based on the technique of photography as a means of fixing images of past events in the present through a flash of light. The work that Hokimoto came up with as a result, is a metaphorical depiction of "the world as a complex entanglement of all kinds of matters." The title was taken from the name of a waste disposal facility in Shimanto, called "Clean Center Ginga." [6] While being a sequel to *Sceneries Outside the Window*, the images in this series were also shot between 2017 and '21, so for the reason explained above, these are again pairs of images in one print, except for the picture of the silk tree. Closeup shots of his niece; gradations of color resulting from the exposure of the film, without discernible concrete motifs; and once again, the silk tree. What is different from *Sceneries Outside the Window*, is that the narrative or semantic connection between these prosaic images is unclear at first sight.

The pictures in *Galaxy* were in fact shot without looking through the camera's finder or at the display. This means that they do not serve the conventional purpose of "records," as not even the photographer himself could predict what would be seen in the resulting photographs.

For understanding *Galaxy*, the one work in this exhibition that offers the fewest clues for objective interpretation, there aren't many other hints than the ambiguous meaning that is given to Galaxy/Ginga here – beautifully shining celestial bodies, and a waste disposal facility as the final destination for things – and the fact that the work follows in the footsteps of *Sceneries Outside the Window* that follows the artist's mother during her final days. What is presented here is the reality after the mother's death, a reality in which "the subject he wanted to capture" no longer exists. It is the very fact that the subject, his mother, is not there anymore, that inspired Hokimoto to express his realization of living in a world in which his mother is absent, by joining together fragments of accidental images that he unexpectedly got hold of. In that sense, it is symbolic that the work starts with images of Hokimoto's niece that represents a new generation, and ends with the same silk tree that is seen in the first picture in the *Sceneries Outside the Window* series that opens this exhibition. Above that, in contrast to the bare tree in the beginning, the silk tree in *Galaxy* have exuberant foliage and even blossoming flowers, which makes one feel the time that has passed up to this point.

On closer reflection, silk trees bloom in early summer, while Hokimoto's mother passed away in the winter. As the photographs in *Galaxy* were taken during the same period as those in *Sceneries Outside the Window*, these images that, positioned at the end of the exhibition, appear to represent sceneries after the mother's death, were in fact taken during her lifetime. This means that the past and the future may be seen as overlapping also in the silk tree that closes the exhibition.

Distance

Once we have understood each of the three works described above, it becomes clear that their contents are interlinked in an organic way. When taking a broader look at the "inter face 1991-2021" exhibition at large, it can be understood as one single work that, in the form of a "montage," sums up several individual works about life and death as events within a family, and about the cycle of the seasons. This is an idea that finally also presents us with a foundation for contemplating on how the works on display reflect in concrete terms the "distance" that Hokimoto aimed to depict.

Regarding the aspect of distance in Hokimoto's work, I metioned above that it is about the gap between the dead and the living. Applied to the works in this exhibition, it becomes evident that its description was primarily executed by regulating "the visualization/non-visualization of the subject to be recorded." Many of the images and footage that appear in Hokimoto's work are casual snapshots of the artist's daily life with his family. On the other hand, the captured sceneries are much larger in number than the average family album of photos or home videos, and in addition, the fact that the artist carried his camera into the hospital and even into the hearse, certainly is another peculiarity. Nonetheless, the way he portrays his mother remains consistent throughout the work. In *Sceneries Outside the Window*, for example, there are no more images showing the mother's face after 50 (p. 29), and her death is communicated to the viewer through scenes of the funeral (62, p. 35).

Quite in contrast to the photographer Nobuyoshi Araki, who once photographed his late wife Yoko even in the coffin after her death, and exhibited the resulting pictures in public, it never occurred to Hokimoto to show his mother's corpse as it was enshrined in the coffin, regardless of whether he actually filmed her. Avoiding direct reference to death, he restricted himself to indirectly describing the loneliness and lostness caused by his mother's death, through scenes before and after the funeral, and places in and outside the house with the mother no longer present.

"The death of a beloved person" is a somewhat commonplace theme that has been addressed by artists of all times and places. Taking this subject and establishing an entirely new form of art around it is not an easy task. Putting aside his great skill as a photographer, if Hokimoto wasn't going to veer over to the directness of Araki, who was in a way undermined by "illness" and had no choice but to take photographs even when that involved tossing away socially-accepted ideas and ethical taboos, all that he could do was to take a step back and remain in an objective position from which he could observe his mother's death. We may also refer to that distance as a "margin." In the case of this exhibition, all the sceneries and characters that have been inserted, including next to the artist's mother also his grandfather, his brother and his niece – and actually also his mother herself, substituted by images – function as the driving forces yet at once also as margins in the story.

At the risk of being misunderstood, I would say that the individual photographs that Hokimoto takes, do not particularly excel in technical terms like composition and focus for example. And yet, in his photos and videos alike, the close relationship with the subject is precisely defined, which is exactly what gives the countless images in this exhibition enough room to permit the viewer's emotional involvement, and thus makes them accessible.

The somewhat disproportionate combination of exquisite placement and continuity, and rather weak images – this amateurish quality, as I would call it, is what helps bridge the distance between the viewer and the images, and allows the viewer to enter into the margins, and thereby sympathize with the narrative at large as a matter of his or her "own concern."

Conclusion

In conventional "art," the morbid, sensational, even thoughtless or taboo-breaking actions of artists, is a kind of behavior that has never really been denied. When considering this, Sora Hokimoto's art seems healthy, ordinary, commonplace. Through the documents that he compiled, he avoided directness in the way he dealt with his mother's death, creating a work of art that maintains a poetic appeal from beginning to end. In other words, he found a way in that narrow margin to share his memories with others – the viewers – while at once shielding his mother from their impertinent gaze. What makes this artist's work so appealing is the way he discovers, extracts, combines and presents the poetic moments within ordinary everyday life, from his own personal point of view.

The fact that Hokimoto, who is at once in the spotlight as a musician, addresses a topic like this, is in itself something that involves the danger of being reduced to an object of empathy and consumption. I am not in a position to criticize the fact that art is being made an object of consumption, however one thing that is quite certain, is that, while many superior works of art aim for immortality, works and activities that win over popular support by eliciting personal sympathy, have in fact a rather short shelf life.

However, while being aware of that risk of becoming an object of consumption himself, Hokimoto acts according to the desire to "capture" the death of a blood relative, and consistently from the time he made *A Song That Never Ends*, he has been processing that sticky desire in a self-referential manner, and converted it into his own style of artistic expression. Maintaining the balance between popularity and artistry without tipping over to either side, and in the end prioritizing the personal feelings that occur within himself, is a practice that, as far as I can tell, defines the underlying character of Hokimoto's creative work at large.

Let me add a comment on a very interesting book that I recently read. It is about bereaved families and how they interpret their dreams of deceased relatives as not "seeing" them actively, but from the passive position of being "shown" the dreams by the respective deceased persons.[7] When considering this, the act of looking out of a window, can be understood as an active behavior that presupposes the will of the acting subject. While this exhibition, put together from actual records, marks the culmination of the artist's search for the distance between the dead – his mother – and himself, which has been ongoing from *Visit Me in My Dreams* through *Sceneries Outside the Window*, it seems at once also as if he has lost sight of his destination. Just like the silk tree in *Galaxy* represent a place that is neither past, present or future, and that is just there with its suggestive notion of possibly announcing the beginning or the end of something. Hokimoto's next challenge is probably to take another step, moving further "out of the window," with all the memories and the painful sense of loss that he feels. His journey will continue, and whenever he looks back on this exhibition, it may appear to him as a new starting point.

---

1 From an interview with Sora Hokimoto that was published in the pamphlet for *Hadaka no yume* (*Visit Me in My Dreams*), 2022, boid inc., pp. 7-8

2 In 1954, large amounts of contaminated tuna were discarded after the Daigo Fukuryu Maru (Lucky Dragon No.5) and many other Japanese fishing boats were contaminated by nuclear fallout from the United States' thermonuclear weapon test at the Bikini and Enewetak atolls in the Marshall Islands.

3 According to a suggestion from the translator of this text, "窓外" in the exhibition title was translated "inter face." Rather than referring to the window (窓) as an "interface," "inter" and "face" are separated here, in order to stress the notion of two different sides "facing" each other, and the physical distance between them.

4 Hokimoto uses an OLYMPUS PEN S camera. However, after digitizing the films, he rearranges the order of the images on his computer, before finally printing them out.

5 *1991* includes picture of the *Hiroshima Panels* by Iri and Toshi Maruki that were taken in 1992 at the Maruki Gallery for The Hiroshima Panels (far right and 3rd from right in the 3rd row, and 3rd from right in the 4th row, p. 58).

6 Ginga (銀河) is the Japanese word for "Galaxy."

7 Kiyoshi Kanebishi, "Koritsu 'mu' en – Why we meet people killed in an earthquake in our dreams," *Watashi no yume made, ai ni kite kureta – 3.11 naki hito to no sore kara* 2021, Asahi Shimbun Publications Inc., pp. 222-242

Reference Literature and Websites

Nobuyoshi Araki (writing, photography), Tokyo Photographic Art Museum (supervision), *Araki Nobuyoshi: Sentimental Journey 1971 – 2017-* (2017, HeHe)

Sora Hokimoto *The Next Chapter – Portraits of Hibakusha in Kochi* (2021, this and that)

Tohoku Gakuin University earthquake documentary project, seminar by Kiyoshi Kanebishi *Watashi no yume made, ai ni kite kureta – 3.11 nakihito to no sorekara* (2021, Asahi Shimbun Publications Inc.)

Hadaka no yume (*Visit Me in My Dreams*) *movie pamphlet (2022, boid inc.)

Sora Hokimoto, *Hadaka no yume* (2023, Shinchosha Publishing Co., Ltd.)

Interview with Sora Hokimoto, director of *A Song That Never Ends* (Text by Takayuki Fukata) https://umi-theater.jimdofree.com/interview-owari/ (last checked February 6, 2024)

Interview with Sora Hokimoto about his idea behind "inter face 1991-2021" and turning documentary photographs into "moving images." (Text by Yuka Kimbara) https://madamefigaro.jp/culture/231229-artistfocus04.html (last checked February 6, 2024)

Filmography

A Song That Never Ends (written and directed by Sora Hokimoto), 2014, 68 minutes
Visit Me in My Dreams (written, directed and edited by Sora Hokimoto), 2022, 59 minutes

Translated by Andreas Stuhlmann

p. 93 〈窓外〉より   From the series *Sceneries Outside the Window*

［展覧会］
ARTIST FOCUS #04
甫木元空　窓外 1991-2021
2023年12月16日 － 2024年2月18日

主催：高知県立美術館（公益財団法人高知県文化財団）
後援：高知県教育委員会、高知市教育委員会、
四万十町、四万十町教育委員会、高知新聞社、
RKC高知放送、KUTVテレビ高知、
KSSさんさんテレビ、KCB高知ケーブルテレビ、
エフエム高知、高知シティFM放送
企画：塚本麻莉（高知県立美術館）
広報物デザイン：重実生哉
映像設計：岩田拓朗（arsaffix Inc.）
会場施工：有限会社カリノ美工

［展覧会カタログ］
ARTIST FOCUS #04
甫木元空　窓外 1991-2021
監修：高知県立美術館

編集：塚本麻莉（高知県立美術館）
執筆：甫木元空、塚本麻莉
デザイン：重実生哉
翻訳：アンドレアス・シュトゥールマン
撮影：高橋洋策（pp. 46-47, 54-55, 64）

発行：高知県立美術館　高知県高知市高須353-2

発売：this and that　愛知県常滑市大野町7-75-1

印刷：弘文印刷株式会社
発行日：2024年3月29日

[Exhibition]
ARTIST FOCUS #04
Sora Hokimoto　inter face 1991-2021
December 16, 2023 – February 18, 2024

Organized by The Museum of Art, Kochi (Kochi Pref.
Foundation for Culture)
Endorsed by Kochi Prefectural Board of Education,
Kochi City Board of Education, Shimanto Town,
Shimanto Town Board of Education, The Kochi Shimbun,
RKC Kochi Broadcasting, TV Kochi Broadcasting,
Kochi SanSan TV, Kochi Cable Broadcast,
FM Kochi Broadcasting, Kochi City FM
Curated by Mari Tsukamoto (The Museum of Art, Kochi)
PR Material Design by Ikuya Shigezane
Video Design by Takuro Iwata (arsaffix Inc.)
Venue Construction by Karinobiko Ltd.

[Exhibition Catalog]
ARTIST FOCUS #04
Sora Hokimoto　inter face 1991-2021
Supervised by The Museum of Art, Kochi

Edited by Mari Tsukamoto (The Museum of Art, Kochi)
Texts by Sora Hokimoto, Mari Tsukamoto
Design by Ikuya Shigezane
Translation by Andreas Stuhlmann
Photography by Hirofumi Takahashi (pp. 46-47, 54-55, 64)

Published by The Museum of Art, Kochi
353-2 Takasu, Kochi City, Kochi Prefecture

Released by this and that
7-75-1 Ohno-cho, Tokoname City, Aichi Prefecture

Printed by Kobun Printing Co., Ltd.
Published on March 29, 2024